Ducks
For Kids
Amazing Animal Books
For Young Readers

By Rachel Smith
Mendon Cottage Books

JD-Biz Publishing

Read More Amazing Animal Books

Purchase at Amazon.com

Download Free Books!
http://MendonCottageBooks.com

Table of Contents

Introduction

Ducks live all over the world, except in Antarctica. They are animals that humans enjoy feeding, raising, and watching.

The duck is an animal that shows up in cartoons as a wacky character; ducks amuse us, with their quacking and their waddling. But did you know that not all ducks quack? Ducks are present in many different tales.

From Hans Christian Anderson's Ugly Duckling to the modern tale of Ping, the duck has been kept in our attention for centuries.

From the Mandarin duck in Asia to the Mallard in America, we have a lot of feathered friends to get to know. Ducks can be a lot more interesting than you would think; from what they eat to how they sound, ducks are different all over the world.

What are ducks?

Duck is not a term that applies to one group. There are several groups of ducks within the same family, called Anatidae, that includes geese and swans. All ducks can fly, but not all are aquatic.

Five white ducks walking.

Ducks are not geese or swans. They are often confused with loons, coots, grebes, and other water birds, but ducks are their own distinct set of groups.

A full grown male duck is called a drake, and a female duck is called a duck, or sometimes a hen. A baby duck, usually one with downy feathers, is called a duckling.

A duck, in essence, is a water bird that belongs to the family Anatidae that has a shorter neck than geese or swans. The majority of the bird family Anatidae is made up of ducks.

They are called ducks because of the way some kinds of ducks 'duck' under the water to eat.

What do ducks look like?

Ducks have long necks compared to other types of birds, but not as long as geese and swans.

A male mallard duck.

Diving ducks tend to have more round bodies as compared to dabbling ducks (more on this in the next chapter). Most ducks have fairly elongated bodies.

They also have webbed feet to help them swim, unlike other birds that just have talons. Since ducks don't land in trees, they don't need to grasp branches.

Ducks also have bills, which are used for eating; ducks also breathe through their bills, with two small nose holes on top. This area is kind of a waxy structure on top of their beaks with most ducks called cere. Another part of their bill is the nail, which is a pointed, hard part on the tip of it.

All ducks have wings, though some aren't very good fliers. Some barely fly at all. Some male ducks have great feathers that make them look fancier than females; a lot of young ducks, almost adults but not quite there, look like females.

Ducks and what they eat

Ducks eat in two different ways: diving and dabbling.

The Baikal teal duck, also known as a bimaculate duck or a squawk duck.

Ducks are easily divided into the two groups of dabbling ducks and diving ducks; this is the easiest way to tell the difference between types of ducks.

Diving ducks are heavier than dabbling ducks, and will dive underwater to get food. They are much more likely to live at sea than dabbling ducks.

Dabbling ducks turn upside down to get food; they tend to be in calmer waters, and their feet are smaller. They eat vegetable matter (plants and such in the water) for the most part. They also eat in shallower water than diving ducks, and are also known as puddle ducks.

Dabbling ducks have pectin in their beaks, which is a strainer to for the water to go through; anything big enough to eat is caught in their beaks, and they swallow it.

Different kinds of ducks eat everything from grasses and vegetable matter to fish, amphibians (like frogs) and molluscs.

How ducks act

There are several things ducks do that do. From daily activities like feeding to less frequent things like molting and migration, ducks do a lot of different things.

Black-bellied whistling tree duck.

Ducks molt their feathers every year. A molt is when feathers come off the bird so new ones can grow; this isn't done all once, because then the duck would be naked and cold!

A duck loses feathers evenly, though sometimes their feathers will appear a little thin. They never have bald spots, and if they do it's not because of molting.

Most ducks migrate every year, from north to south and back again. This is to avoid the cold weather that winter brings; most ducks aren't made to survive freezing winters.

A duck knows south from north, and can navigate from its place in the north to its place in the south and back again without any assistance. This is unlike humans, who don't have a built in system to tell the directions from each other. Humans need maps to find a specific place most of the time; ducks do not. Young ducks are taught the way there by their parents, and after that point it's memorized, meaning they remember it no matter what.

Ducks are only mates for about a year before they move on to the next mate. They usually breed once a year, and make a nest for their ducklings before they are laid.

They lay eggs, and when the eggs hatch, the ducklings are immediately brought to the water by the mother.

If a duckling is trapped somewhere away from its mother, sometimes the mother will leave it behind. A mother duck may also leave behind a duckling if it's sickly or a runt.

Ducks and humans

Ducks have been domesticated (made friendly to humans) for thousands of years. It's thought that they may have been domesticated first in Southeast Asia, though no one knows for sure.

Domestic ducks eating feed.

Humans keep ducks for meat, eggs, and feathers. They're very similar to chickens in that way, but in the Western world (Europe and America), chickens are cheaper to keep than ducks, and also have more lean meat. So, duck meat is considered more of a delicacy (treat) than chicken meat.

Ducks are considerably more popular in China.

Domestic ducks have a very hard time sitting on their own eggs. Typically, if a farmer wants to hatch ducklings, they have to get a hen to sit on it, or put them in an incubator.

Duck eggs from domestic ducks are blue-green to white in color. They are also not that different in size from chicken eggs.

Some ducks are also kept as pets; these ducks need a place to swim, whether it's a deep water dish or a pond. Domestic ducks will usually eat insects, frogs, and other animals it can scavenge from the pond. They also need a coop to live in to protect them from predators.

Mallards

Mallard ducks are the ducks from which almost all domestic ducks come from.

A group of mallard ducks.

A mallard is a species of duck that lives all over the world in temperate (kind of warm) and subtropical (warm, but not as warm as tropical) climates. It lives in North Africa, North America, Europe, Asia, and South America naturally. It's also been brought to Australia and New Zealand.

Mallards are colored differently from males to females. Males have green, shiny heads and brown wings, and females are brown and speckled all over.

The interesting thing about mallards is that they can breed with some other species of ducks, and hybrid ducks can be born fully able to live and function.

Mallards live in wetlands, and they can be either fresh water or salt water. Mallards from North America typically fly south to Mexico for the winter.

When the female is nesting, she needs a space with easy food and that is hidden from predators. This is because she lays more than half her body weight in eggs! She can easily get stressed out about nesting, and so it's important that there aren't extra stressors.

Mallards are very adaptable, meaning they can live in environments that some other animals and ducks might not be able to. For example, mallards have adjusted well to human-created environments; some even live indoors in hotels!

They also tend to create a problem with local wildlife, because they can breed with local ducks and are so adaptable. They tend to make things harder for other ducks and waterfowl.

This is called 'genetic pollution' because they slowly destroy the breeds of ducks that are already there by mating with them and having hybrids. A hybrid with mallards can still have babies, unlike other species that interbreed, like tigers and lions. If too many hybrid babies are born instead of the local ducks, then it can cause a problem with the local ducks continuing on.

The other thing about interbreeding with mallards is that the hybrids are often bigger. This means they need more food, and this can cause a problem too.

Muscovy ducks

Muscovy ducks live mainly in Mexico, Central America, and South America. They also live in some places in the United States of America, though they aren't quite native to that area.

A pair of Muscovy ducks.

Muscovy ducks have a wattle on their beak, unlike a lot of other ducks. They also have long claws, and the males are about twice the size of the females. The area covering the top of their beak and part of their face is nude, meaning that it doesn't have any feathers; it can be red or red and black.

No one is sure why Muscovy ducks are called that; the name means 'from Moscow' which is a city in Russia far, far away from their native habitat.

The Muscovy duck has been domesticated, and it is sometimes referred to as a Barbary duck in some areas; in others, it's only referred to as a Barbary duck if it's been cooked and ready to eat. Native American tribes first domesticated the Muscovy duck, though they called them by a different name.

An interesting thing about Muscovy ducks is that they do not migrate. They can handle very low temperatures, and usually their habitat does not get extremely cold as, say, in Canada. The fact they can handle pretty low temperatures is why they are settling down in America and even Canada.

Unlike mallards, the Muscovy duck doesn't make a stable pair when mating. Instead, the mother is left to lay eggs and take care of them on her own. The father doesn't stay to help and leaves shortly after the eggs are fertilized (meaning that they have babies in them).

Muscovy ducks outside of their habitat are a species that are causing a problem in America and even in the United Kingdom across the sea. Muscovy ducks don't have natural predators in those areas, and they reproduce fairly quickly, so they take away the food of local ducks. They are considered a pest.

Muscovy ducks don't quack, though they do make noise. Their meat is liked better than mallard or other domestic ducks, and for this reason they are popular as domesticated animals.

While it's not legal to trade live Muscovy ducks (to other places, like from country to country), it is legal to trade the meat.

A duck that is a hybrid of Muscovy duck and mallard is called a mulard duck and can't have babies, like a mule. These ducks are often eaten by Israelis (people from Israel in the Middle East) because they are considered kosher, or good to eat according to the rules for food in Judaism, the religion of Israelis.

Ring-necked ducks

Ring-necked ducks are diving ducks. They live in North America, and are small or medium sized.

A male ring-necked duck.

Unlike Muscovy ducks, the males are only a little bigger than the females. They look a lot alike, but females are browner and less vibrantly colored than the males.

Because they have white rings around their bill, and their neck ring can be kind of hard to see, they are sometimes called ringbills instead of ring-necked ducks. They also have an angular head, which means it's an unusual shape compared to a lot of other ducks.

They eat plants, both under water and above water, but ducklings tend to eat things like insects and worms. Adults eat things like wild rice.

Ducks pair off in the spring as they migrate; when they reach breeding grounds, any ducks that aren't paired off will not have a mate that year. The female of a pair will lay one egg a day. She usually does this until all the eggs are laid, and then she takes care of the eggs.

The pairs never stay together after breeding. It's up to the female to take care of the ducklings.

Sometimes, this type of duck will migrate all the way to Britain or Ireland; this is known as vagrancy, because it isn't their natural pattern. It's very rare that they migrate to Britain, but it happens almost every year.

Mandarin ducks

Mandarin ducks are ducks that live primarily in Asia, in particular East Asia. They are very pretty, striking ducks.

A male and a female mandarin duck.

One of the interesting things about mandarin ducks is that they are perching ducks. Unlike most kinds of duck, this duck will land high in trees and perch there.

The adult male is the one will all the color in its plumage. Like many other types of bird, it uses this color to attract mates; the more colorful, the better.

Mandarin ducks have a smaller population nowadays than they used to; because of destruction of their habitat and exportation (meaning that they are traded to somewhere outside of the country), the numbers have dwindled. However, mandarin ducks are not endangered, and there are still a good number of them living in the wild.

Mandarin ducks eat by dabbling, or else by walking on land. They eat things like seeds and plants, but it really depends on the season. In the summer, they'll eat more things like frogs, worms, and small snakes. When it's winter or fall, they tend to eat things like acorns and grains because there isn't as much available to eat.

The Chinese refer to the mandarin duck as yuan-yang, and they are symbols of fidelity and life-long love. This is because they are perceived to stay together as a pair their whole lives.

A similar representation is felt in Korea as well; they are often given as gifts in Korean weddings.

Pink-eared ducks

Pink-eared ducks are an Australian kind of duck; they have wide bills and are sometimes called zebra ducks due to their stripes.

Pink Eared Duck Wikimedia Commons

They are called pink-eared ducks because of a small pink spot that is in the corner of the black on their heads. However, this spot is hard to see at a distance.

The pink-eared duck is covered in black and white stripes, and also has a black eye patch on each side of its head. Its relatives are extinct, making it a fairly unique and peculiar bird.

It has been considered a perching duck, but it's unsure which family it belongs to. It's certainly not related to the mandarin duck, despite both of their landing in trees.

Pink-eared ducks can live anywhere there is standing water, meaning water staying fairly still. They eat plankton and other small animals, using their bills to strain them.

Another thing they do to feed is create a vortex; two ducks spin around a point with one's head facing the other's tail, and it makes a sort of column where food (plankton and such) is trapped.

Hottentot teals

Hottentot teals are a kind of duck that live in Africa.

A hottentot teal.

This duck tends to live in places like Nigeria and Madagascar, though it migrates to and from Nigeria and other places in north Africa, and it is sedentary (meaning it doesn't migrate) in western Africa and Madagascar.

One thing about hottentot teals is that they have babies all year round. It depends on rainfall, however; if there hasn't been enough, they won't try to have babies.

The young ducklings leave the nest very soon after hatching, and the mother doesn't do so much for them after that; her job is to warn them of predators and protect them, as well as lead them to areas to get food.

A hottentot teal will typically build its nest above ground in something like a tree stump.

They are not endangered.

'Teal' is a name applied to many of the ducks in the Anas genus (which includes mallards). However, there is no particular definition of what makes a duck a teal.

Swans

Swans are the largest members of Anatidae. They are also some of the largest flying birds.

A white swan.

While related to ducks, swans are very much not ducks. They have much longer necks and bigger bodies; they also have teeth, some of the few birds to have any.

Swans tend to eat frogs and fish, and they don't dabble like many ducks do. Their young are called swanlings or cygnets, and an adult male is a cob. A female adult swan is called a pen.

A lot of northern swans are white, but there are also black and black-and-white swans. A lot of swans have black beaks, but some also have orange, and others still have red.

Swans don't live in the tropics, instead preferring temperate climates (like the Northern United States, for example).

They often mate for life, with swans having been recorded living together as a pair from as young as 20 months of age. This is in spite of the fact that swans can only have babies from about four to seven years old and onwards.

There are only about 6-7 types of swans, as compared to the multitudes of ducks.

A swan is a beautiful creature, and closely related to the duck (as well the goose). But it's important to remember they definitely are not ducks.

Geese

Geese are also a relative of ducks, and usually larger than them. However, they are smaller than swans most of the time.

A Canadian goose.

Geese are in the subfamily Anserinae, and the tribe Anserini. There are three genera (or types) of geese: Chen (or white geese), Anser (or gray geese) and Branta (or black geese).

An example of a type of goose is the Canadian goose, which is native to North America. It also migrates sometimes to Europe, and lives in some other parts of the world, such as Britain, due to being introduced there.

Canadian geese are Branta, or black geese, because of their black heads. They migrate in a V-shaped formation, and mostly eat plants.

Geese have been domesticated for a long time. In fact, no one remembers when geese were first domesticated. Geese are kept for similar reasons as ducks: meat, feathers, and eggs. Domestic geese are all descended from the swan goose, which is a gray goose.

Geese are also similar to ducks, but their necks are longer and they are more vicious in fighting away possible predators. They are not ducks, even though they are closely related.

Conclusion

Ducks have been around for thousands, possibly millions of years. They will probably be around for much, much longer, since they adapt so well.

We enjoy the duck, from feeding them for fun to watching them in cartoons. Ducks are friendlier than geese and swans, and we enjoy having them as pets and farm animals.

Ducks are amazing creatures, and we're lucky to have them.

Author Bio

Rachel Smith is a young author who enjoys animals. Her family had fish for about half of her childhood, including a large pink kissing gourami that liked to nibble at the other fish. Once, she had a rabbit who was very nervous. She's also had several pet mice, who were the funniest little animals to watch. She doesn't like dogs ever since a wild one bit her brother on the hand. She lives in Ohio with her family and writes in her spare time. She's also trained as a dental assistant.

Our books are available at

1. Amazon.com

2. Barnes and Noble

3. Itunes

4. Kobo

5. Smashwords

6. Google Play Books

Download Free Books!
http://MendonCottageBooks.com

Publisher

JD-Biz Corp

P O Box 374

Mendon, Utah 84325

http://www.jd-biz.com/

www.ingramcontent.com/pod-product-compliance
Lightning Source LLC
Chambersburg PA
CBHW050850290526
45792CB00002B/603